Teaching Kids to Draw

REALISTICALLY

(AND ALSO CRAZY ADULTS WHO THINK THEY CAN'T!)

By Jacqui Grantford

Cover image drawing © Jacqui Grantford

Cover image hand photograph© Zheltobriukh | Megapixl.com

www.jacquigrantford.com

ISBN-13: 978-0-646-98251-9

www.theartofteaching.com.au

Book cover and layout by Sarah Messina

CONTENTS

ABOUT THIS BOOK

This book is designed to help teachers formulate activities and exercises that will naturally teach students to observe the world around them.

The exercises are suited for any age, including adults, however, if you are teaching younger children, have them draw simple subjects. It also helps if they are drawing something they are interested in.

The later chapters in the book that focus on perspective, foreshortening and proportions are more suited to students from the age of 8 and up. But it is surprising how even younger children will catch on to ideas, so simplified versions of these more difficult topics can still be beneficial to them.

As your students are learning, always encourage them to look at what is in front of them and not to worry if it doesn't match up with how they think something 'should' look.

Encourage them to trust that if they follow the lines and curves without questioning, then it will come together in the end. And each time they do, their drawing will get better and better.

ABOUT THE AUTHOR

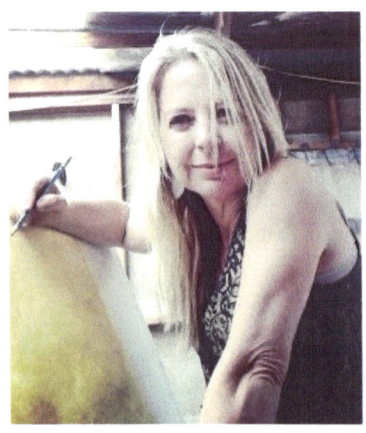

I have been passionate about art my entire life and have worked extensively as an artist, children's book illustrator, author and educator. As a child, creating art was my greatest joy, and I would spend hours drawing and painting. My friends in primary school would ask me to draw things for them, and I always felt that art was my 'thing'. Nothing really changed as an adult, and I'm still colouring in!

I started running after-school art classes and have been working with children for 30 years. During this time I worked out the most effective ways to transfer my knowledge of art and how to draw to kids. I had to break down what I did naturally and try and work out how to translate that into simple exercises that would help children develop the ability to draw realistically.

And I discovered that with the right direction and encouragement and with plenty of practice drawing from life, just about every student can develop drawing skills. I believe we should encourage children to draw from a young age, not only from their imaginations but also from observation.

Here are samples of my own artwork.

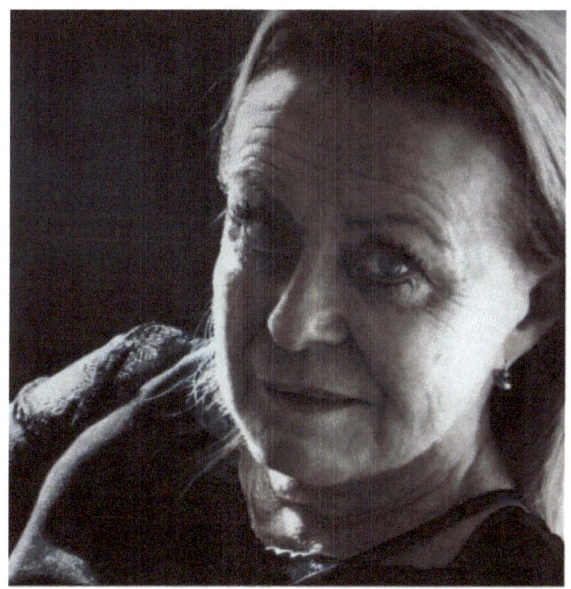

Oil on linen, 120 x 120 cm

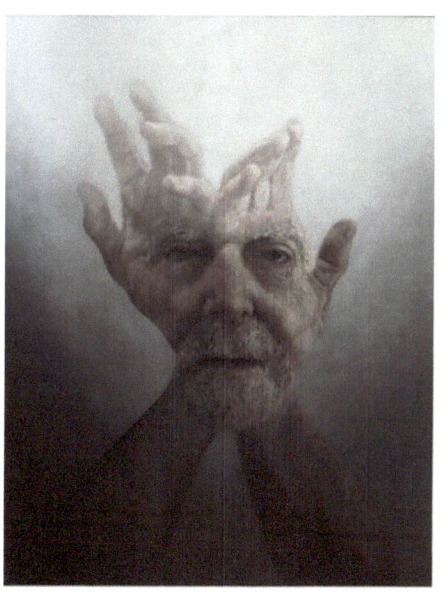

Oil on board, 120 x 97 cm

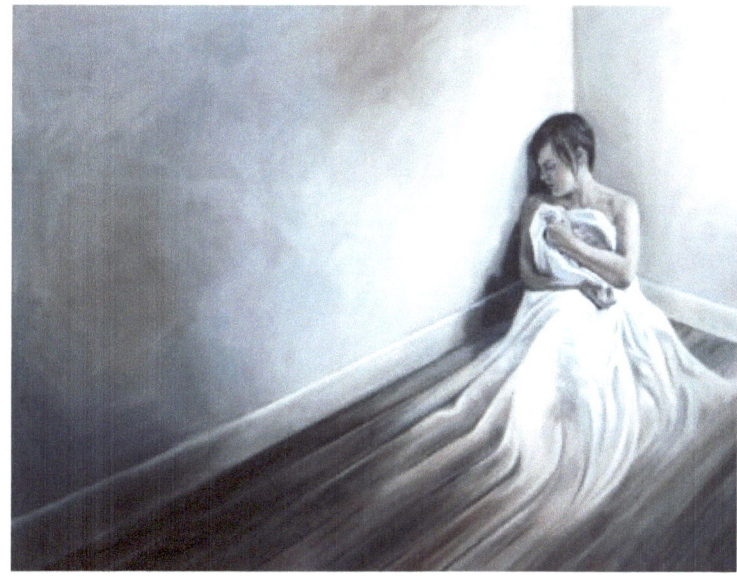

Oil on canvas, 100 x 77 cm

INTRODUCTION

I can't even draw a stick figure!

How many times have we heard that catchphrase? It's something that develops from the age of 8 onwards with many children and continues into adulthood. And yet when children are very young, they never question the fact that they CAN draw.

So what happens to make children suddenly stop believing in their ability to draw and paint?

They lose self-belief at about the same time that creating a realistic representation of what they want to draw becomes important.

Prior to that, it's not such a big deal, and kids are more than happy to be creating from their imaginations and following their natural progression.

But when they want to draw realistically and the tools aren't there they become disillusioned.

All they need is direction and to be shown how.

And that's where this book can help!

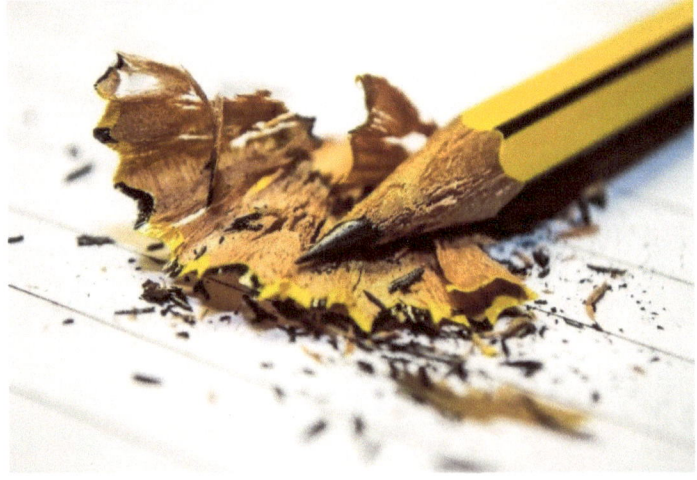

STAGES OF DEVELOPMENT

Let's have a look at the natural stages of development that children go through in their ability to draw.

Children start scribbling at about one or two years of age. This is when you have to really watch those walls for accidental artworks around the house!

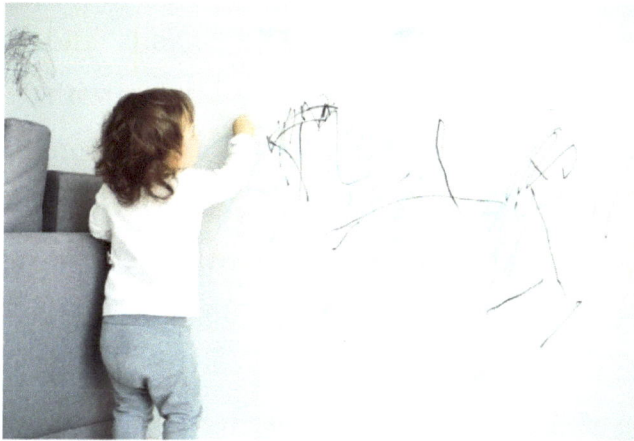

© Mcloud | Megapixl.com

They use sweeping motions and sometimes lines go off the page.

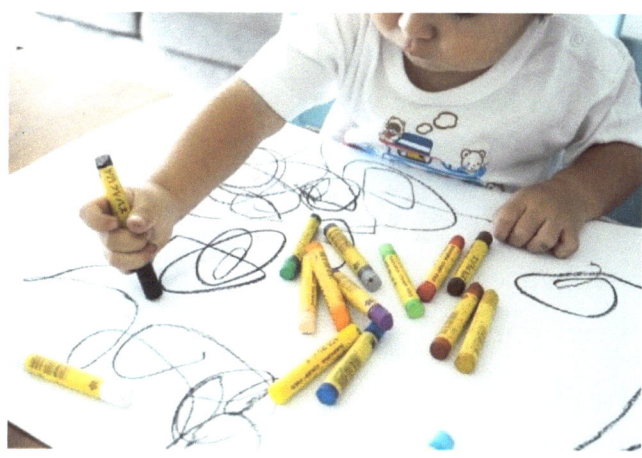

Next, representational shapes and figures emerge around the age of three or four.

People are drawn as circles with sticks coming out. Parts are missing, and they look a little like tadpoles.

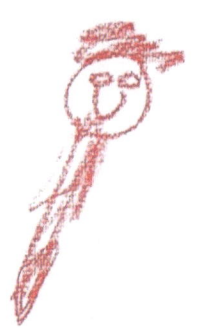

From about five to seven, they use graphic symbols to represent things they encounter in their environment.

When drawing people, they usually have big heads with little hands and feet. The body is drawn with two lines rather than a single line. It's a static pose with arms out and always front on; they don't think to depict people in profile.

The sky is drawn as a single line with a big, happy, yellow sun.

They don't overlap things. For example, if doing a still life, all the objects are typically spaced separately on the page.

Around the age of eight to ten, children strive towards optical realism in their drawings. This is when the trouble can start, and children can give up art through frustration if they don't think their drawings look real.

They put lots of details in their work, especially figures, including teeth and eyelashes (but they rarely remember the eyelids!). Noses are drawn with very obvious nostrils and lines.

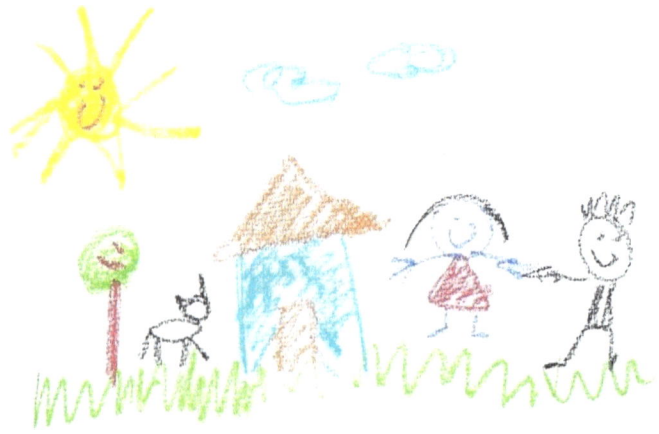

The reason that children are not able to draw in a realistic style as they get older is often that they haven't been shown how!! Some students will naturally pick it up and know instinctively 'how to see'. But for most, it's a mystery.

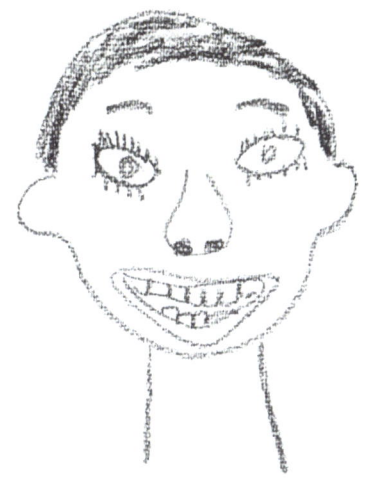

Prior to this age, kids have been continuously encouraged to draw from their imaginations. Why don't you draw a big castle, or why don't you draw what you did on your holidays? They're encouraged to look to their memory as to how things look in their mind, and naturally, they choose the most common appearance of any subject and develop a language of symbols.

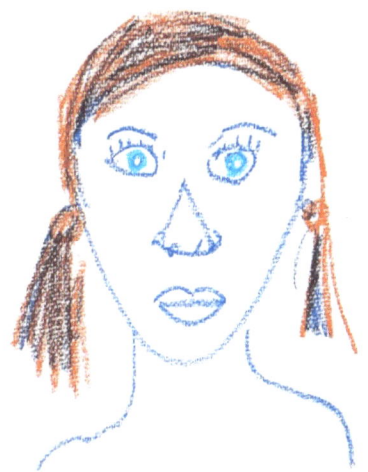

Even the most experienced artist would struggle to get complete realism drawing only upon their memory, but this is the expectation that kids (and adults) put upon themselves.

There's very little instruction advising children to go and choose something that they can see and copy it. We somehow feel that would be diminishing the child's imagination. But if anyone wants to draw realistically, that's precisely what they have to do.

Choose what they want to draw and then copy it – from life or a photo. It's that simple.

And if kids are encouraged to do this from a young age, then when they're older, they will already have an understanding of how to draw realistically.

You would never ask a child to play a Mozart Concerto on the piano without formal training. And yet that's what we expect with art. With music, some children will naturally be able to play by ear, just as some instinctively know how to draw. But for the most part, kids need to be shown.

As we continue to draw from our memory, it becomes harder to tell apart 'what we see' from 'what we think we see'.

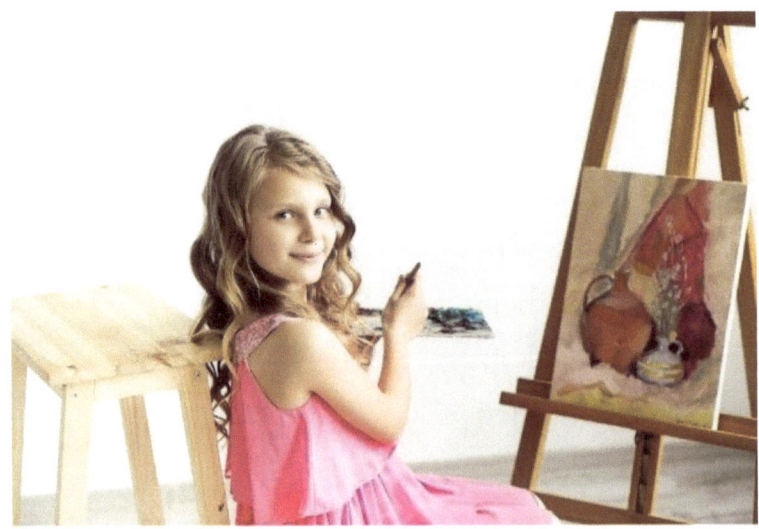

© Natazhekova | Megapixl.com

START DRAWING FROM LIFE

The very first thing to do when teaching children how to draw realistically is to get them drawing from life. This can start at any age.

Pick some flowers from the garden to draw, or visit an interesting location and ask the children to observe what is in front of them and draw it. And point out to them anything that might look a little unusual. Ask them to draw portraits of their friends in profile and before they even start, point out that the eye will look different side on to front on.

And most importantly, tell them not to worry if it doesn't immediately look the way they think it should.

Emphasise that it's like a jigsaw puzzle, and often the drawing will only make sense when it's all put together.

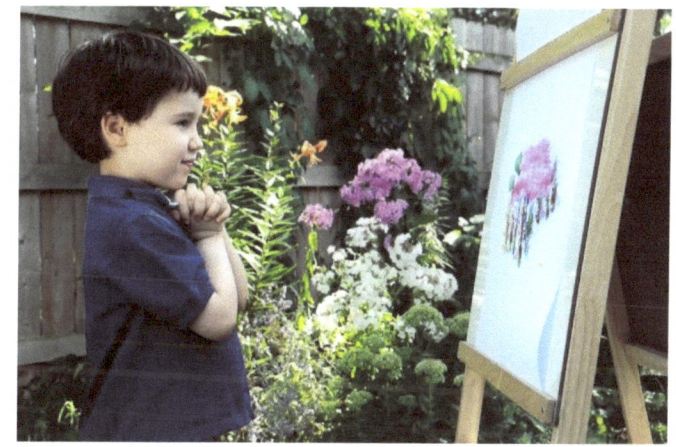

© Rossario | Megapixl.com

Ask the children to draw figures in unusual poses, so they have to really think about how the person looks in those poses.

If you do this, you are beginning the process of training children to look at what is in front of them, and to draw what they see, rather than symbols.

And this process can begin at any age. Even adults who have lost faith in their ability to draw can learn if they start to look at things and forget how they think they 'should' look.

COPYING SIMPLE THINGS
FIRST

Sometimes our brains have convinced us that some things are harder to draw than others. It's actually not true. Everything is just a series of lines of varying lengths, curves and angles with some shading in the mix.

But as much as we tell our brain this fact it won't always listen.

So it can be good to start simple.

For instance, copying simple graphic designs is an effective way of training your eye to imitate the angle and length of what is in front of you. And because it's something abstract we don't put that pressure on ourselves to make it look real.

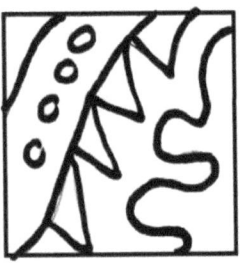 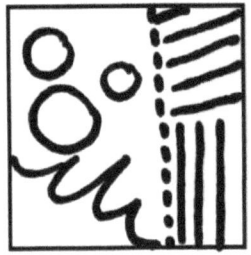

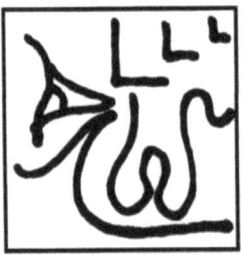

Here are some samples of some graphic designs for students to copy.
Change the level of complexity depending on the age and ability of the students.

SWITCHING THE ANGLE AROUND

Once the students have become confident at copying simple abstract designs, give them some simple drawings or comic characters and ask them to draw them upside down. I used to get students to draw Spot the dog upside down, and the kids would be so thrilled when they turned it the right way around and saw how well they had done. They then had the confidence to draw Spot the right way up, and the result was much more accurate than if they hadn't drawn it upside down first.

Betty Edwards talks about this in her book 'Drawing from the Right Side of the Brain'. I was delighted when I read many of the strategies she writes about, and discovered they were things that I had been doing with students already throughout my teaching. (I would highly recommend her book!)

After they have done some drawings upside down, ask the students to draw some side on, to keep their brains flexible as they look at the lines with fresh eyes.

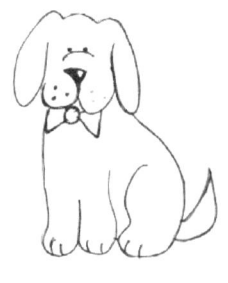
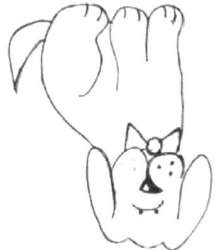

Here is a simple dog for the students to draw upside down. I haven't used Spot the dog here as an example for copyright reasons, but if you choose something the students can relate to, they will love it even more and feel they have achieved success when they can draw it accurately.

THE DETAIL WITHIN

If children are asked to draw the detail within something, they will often panic and not be able to decipher it. Their minds are running a script about what they think they should be seeing.

For this exercise, we are going to ask them to draw a design similar to our previous activities. This design will be the interior detail of something, but we won't tell the students that.

In the example shown here, it's the detail in a hand that's at an unusual angle. Once they have drawn the detail accurately, we will give them a drawing of the whole hand to draw, and this time the detail will be much simpler for them. They will start to break down the barriers of how they think the hand should look and how it actually does at this angle.

Here are two samples of the detail within a subject.
Can you guess what they may end up being?
This is also fun for the students to do.

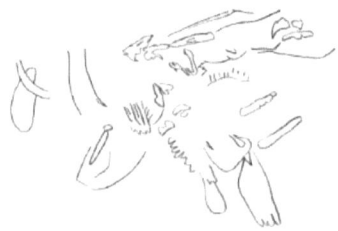

After the students have drawn the interior, give them the rest of the image to copy and fill in the outside.

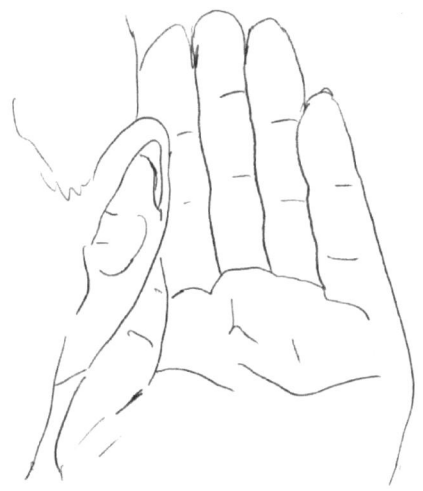

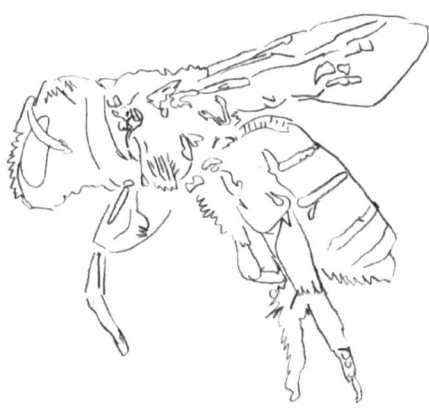

BRING IN THE SHADING

Introduce the students to cross-hatching.

This is when the lines of the shading change direction. If you were shading a square, you might shade it diagonally first, then go over it in the opposite direction. Then horizontally and vertically. You keep doing this until you have a perfectly smooth result.

It requires practice to hone the fine motor skills necessary to control the pencil enough to obtain a smooth transition.

Quite often, students won't have enough variation in their shading when they start, or they will have everything shaded too dark without enough highlights.

Give them five squares to shade that are joined in a row. Tell them that the left square should be as dark as they can get it, the right square as light, and the middle squares gradients.

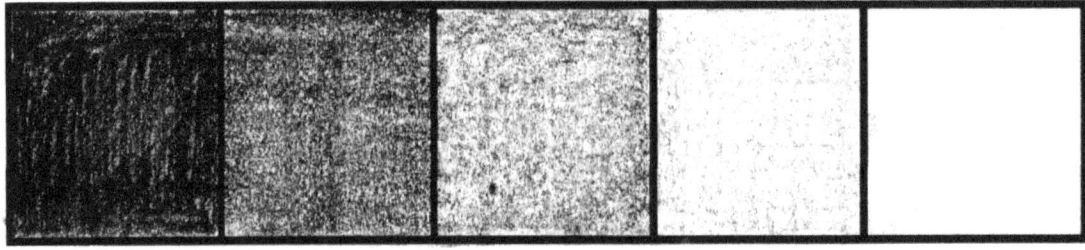

Also, get them practising an exercise where one side of the page is the darkest shading they can do, the other side is white, and the middle is a mid-tone. They have to make them all transition as smoothly as possible, this time without the squares.

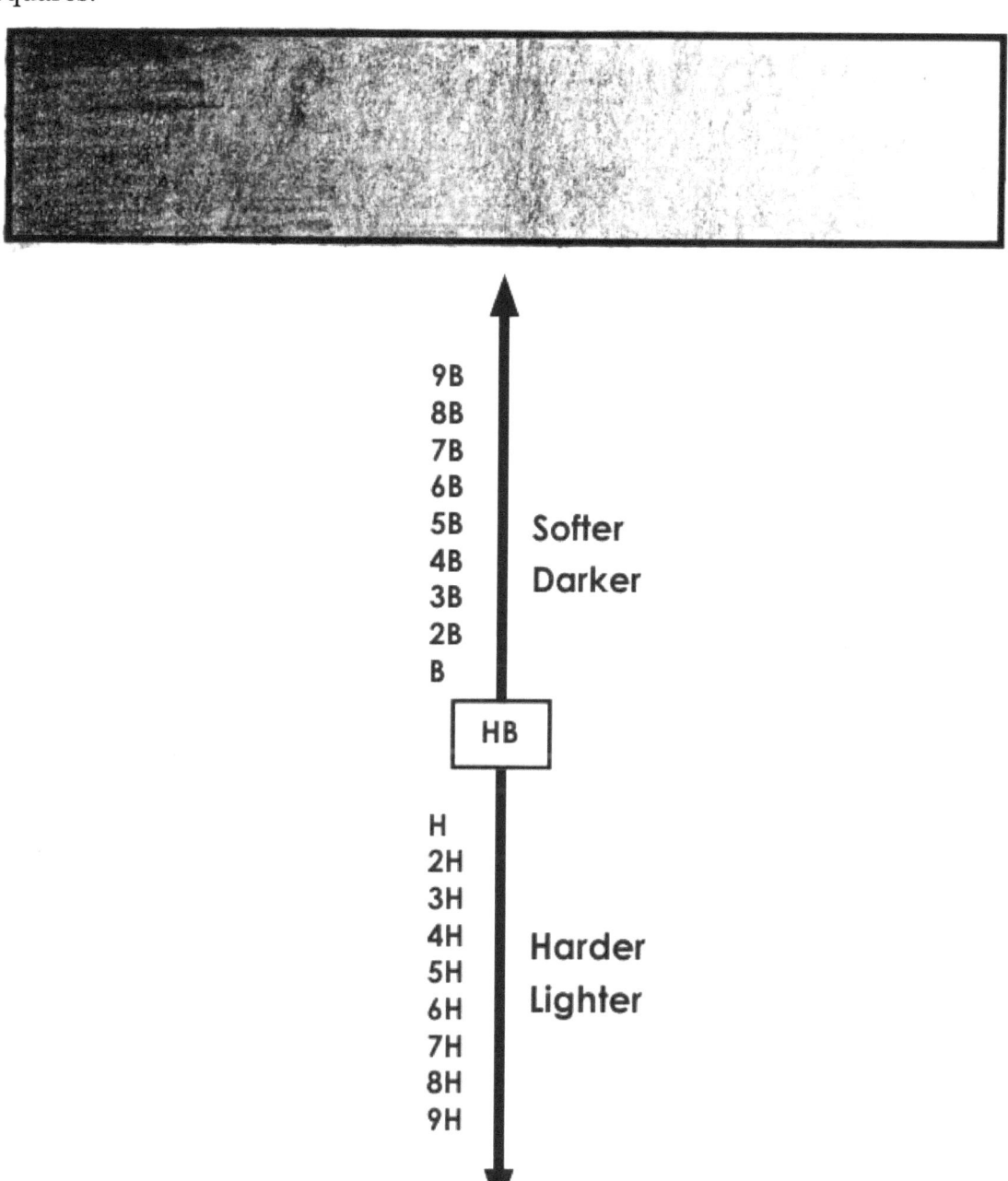

Once the students have a good mastery of these exercises, give them similar designs to the ones that they copied the lines from, but this time ask them also to add shading using cross-hatching and to vary the strength of their pencil pressure.

Ask the students to choose a side that will always be the lightest to shade.

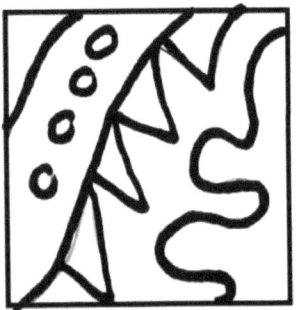 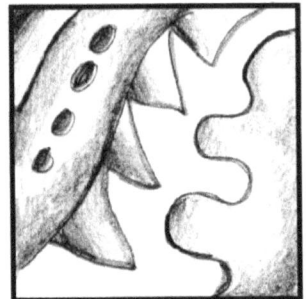

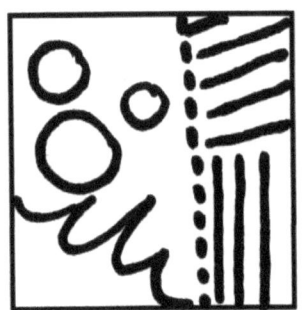 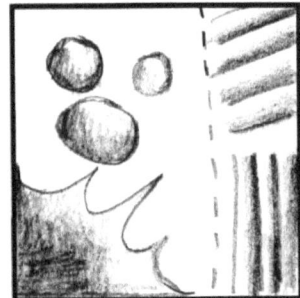

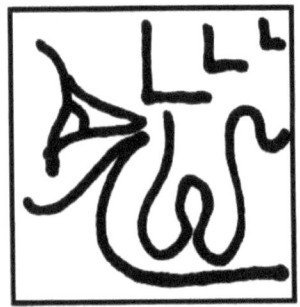 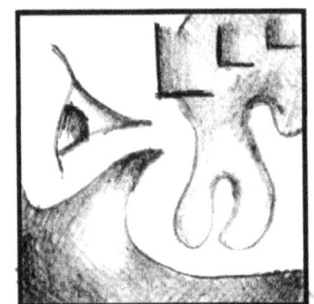

Next, practise shading spheres and shapes to develop skills transitioning from light to dark.

It requires practice to hone the fine motor skills necessary to control the pencil enough to obtain a smooth transition.

Now take what the students were drawing in the previous activity and bring in shading to develop the look of something 3D. Tell them not to worry if it doesn't look exactly right. They're just exploring tone and shape at this stage.

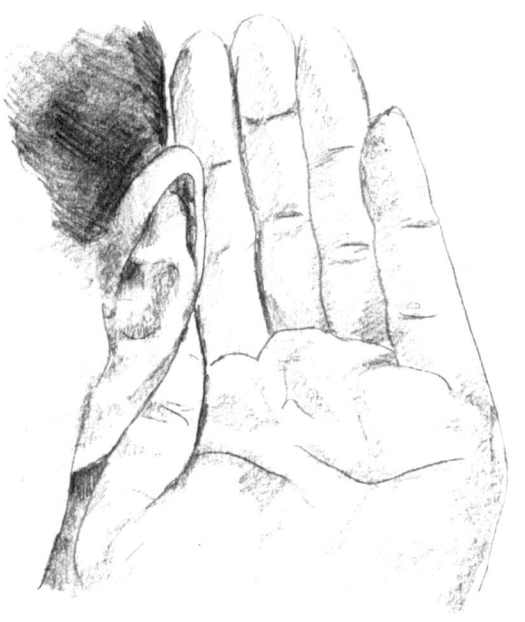

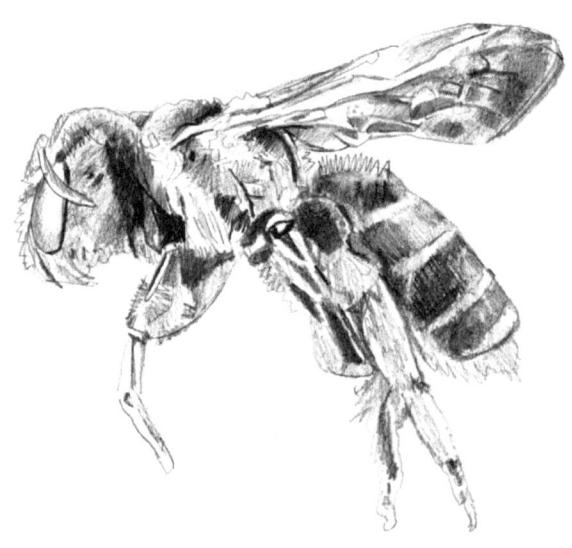

DIFFERENT TYPES OF PENCILS

Another important technique is to learn is how to vary the strength of pressure with a single pencil.

Pencils come in a variety of tones from dark to light.

These are the most common.

Dark < 8B 6B 4B 2B B HB F 2H 4H 6H > Light

Ask the students to experiment with them and play with the different effects. Then give them a sheet of paper with five blank squares, each with a different shading exercise.

SHADE IN THE BOXES BELOW USING THE DIFFERENT PENCILS AND PRESSURE

Shade as dark as you can with 6B

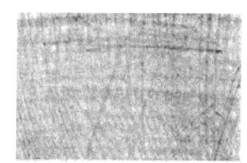

Shade as dark as you can with 2H

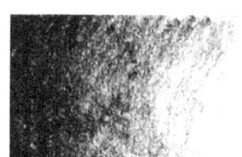

Shade from as dark as you can
to as light as you can with 6B

Shade from as dark as you can
to as light as you can with 2H

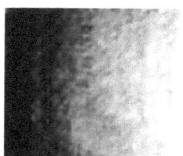

Shade from as dark as you can to as light as
you can with 6B then go over it with 2H

Also, experiment with shading on the side of the pencil as well as the point. The side is great for blocking in large areas, and the point for adding detail.

Ask the students to create a design where half of it is plain with large blocks of area to shade with the side of the pencil, and the other half is detailed and will need the point of the pencil to draw and shade in the fine parts.

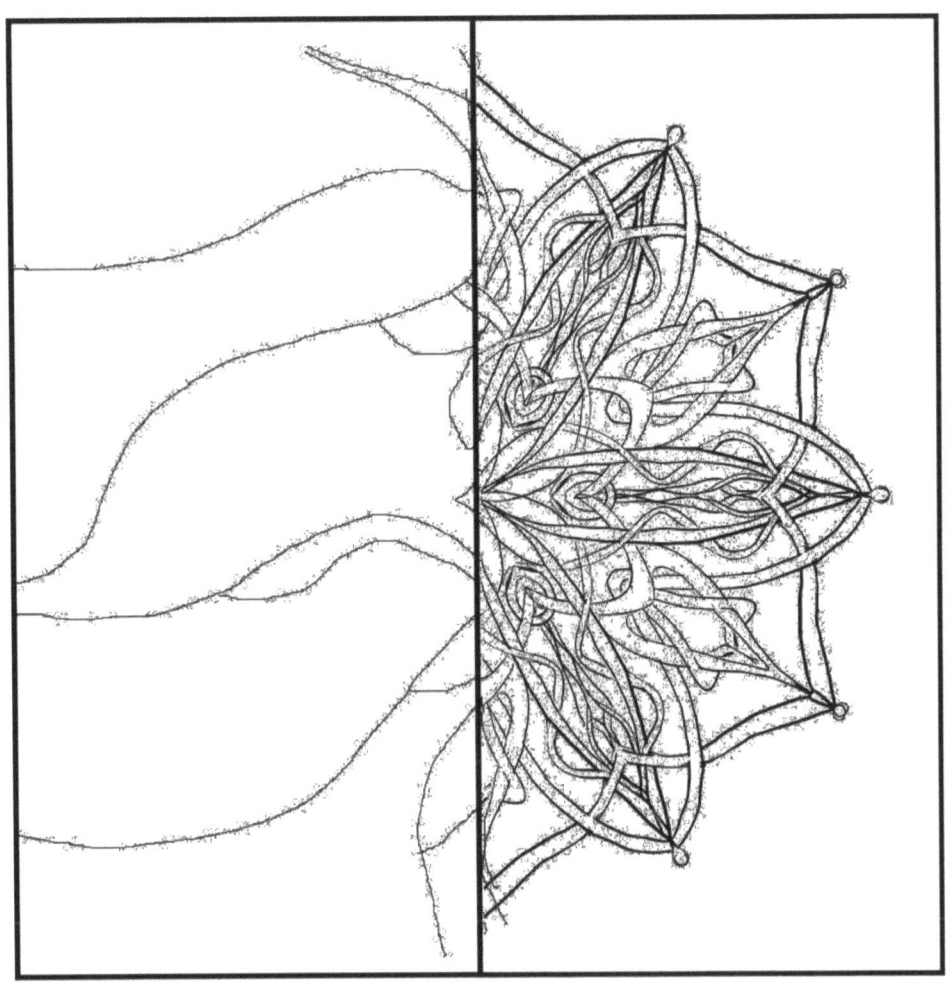

Plain half with side of pencil   Pattern half with point of pencil

GRIDS ON PHOTOGRAPHS

This exercise is a step up from copying the abstract designs. Copying from photos can help to train our eye.

Draw a simple grid over the photo that your students are going to copy. (Pick something they like! Flowers may not be their thing, but they're suitable for this demonstration.)

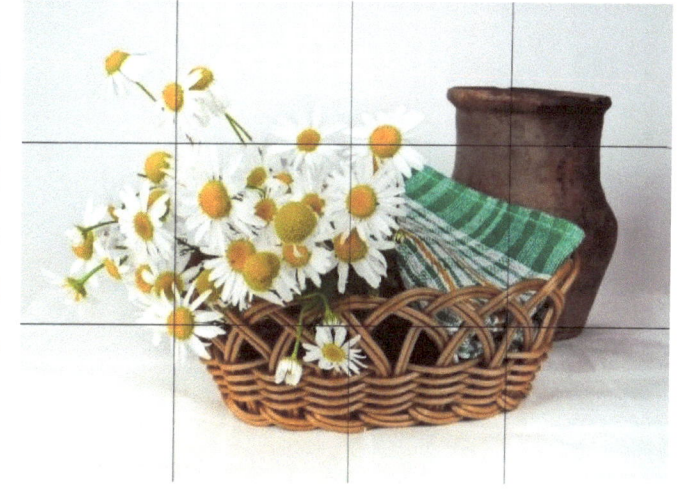

Please don't make it too many squares or they will spend the whole time counting up and down. The grid helps the kids think about the placement and turns each little section into an abstracted part.

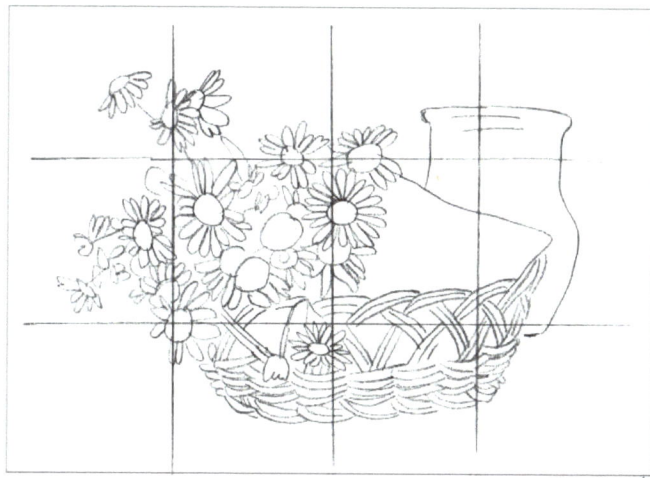

Get the students to do a drawing that's exactly the same size as the photo first, using only line and not using any shading at this stage.

Then get them to practise drawing it double the size, so they get used to the idea of measuring ratio and comparing the size of things to each other.

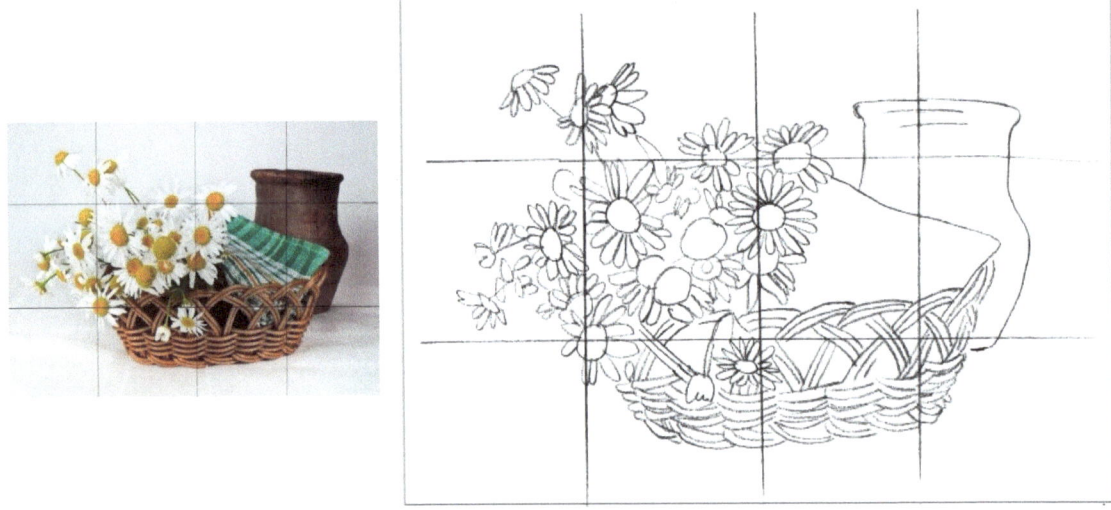

They can finish it off with a bit of shading.

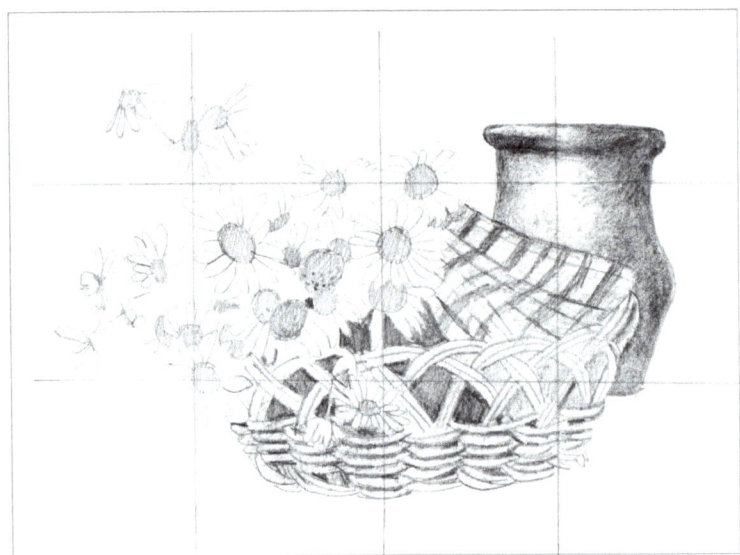

The adventurous students can then copy the photos without the grids if they like.

GRIDS ON REAL-LIFE

Create a measuring frame and draw a grid on it. You can buy a picture frame and turn that into one.

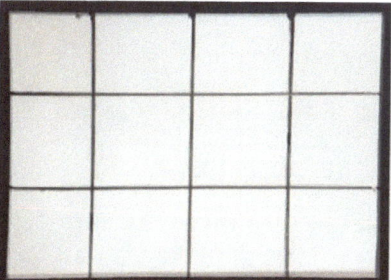

Now set up a simple still-life. Ask the students to hold the frame in front of the still life and draw it onto the glass with a whiteboard marker.

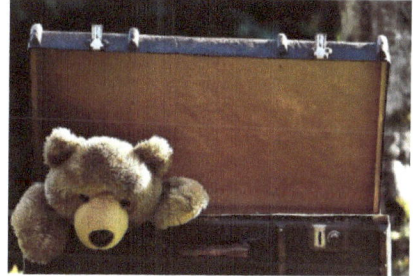 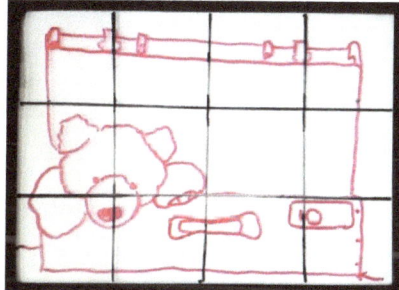

They can then transfer that onto their paper and shade the rest of the drawing.

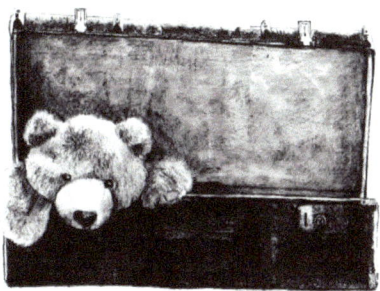

After this, ask the students to hold the grid in front of a different still-life. And then to draw straight onto their paper that also has the grid lightly drawn on it.

DRAWING LIKE CHUCK CLOSE

Chuck Close is an American painter, artist and photographer who achieved fame as a photorealist through his massive-scale portraits. He suffers from prosopagnosia (face blindness, so he can't recognise different people's faces). But through working from a gridded photograph, he builds his images without needing to see the whole face or who the person is.

So even though he can't recognise faces, he can still create an amazing likeness through this technique. We are going to take the grid idea and develop it a little.

The first activity is ideal for a group if you have several students learning. Blow up a picture of what you're going to draw and photocopy it into sections that are A4 each. Then give each student only one of the sections. It won't make any sense to the student and will probably seem like an abstracted image.

Each student copies their section as closely as they can. Once they're all done, join them up to create a single image. Through doing this, they will see how the whole is made up of little parts that don't necessarily make sense on their own.

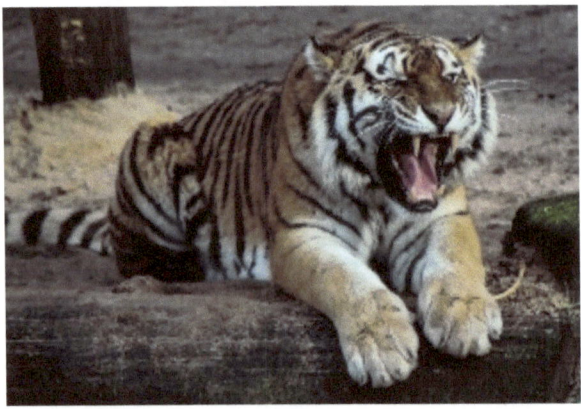

Here is our initial picture that's been enlarged to 120 x 84 cm.

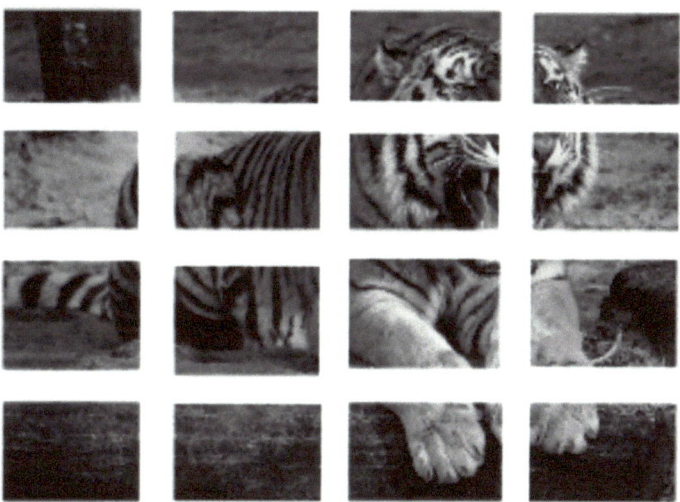

Each student gets an A4 photocopy of only the part that they must copy. Don't tell the students what it is part of, so they get a lovely surprise when it's put together. Once each section is drawn, put them all together to create the single image. It won't match perfectly but will look wonderfully interesting.

And the students will get a surprisingly realistic result, by only focusing on a section and not worrying about how the whole thing looks.

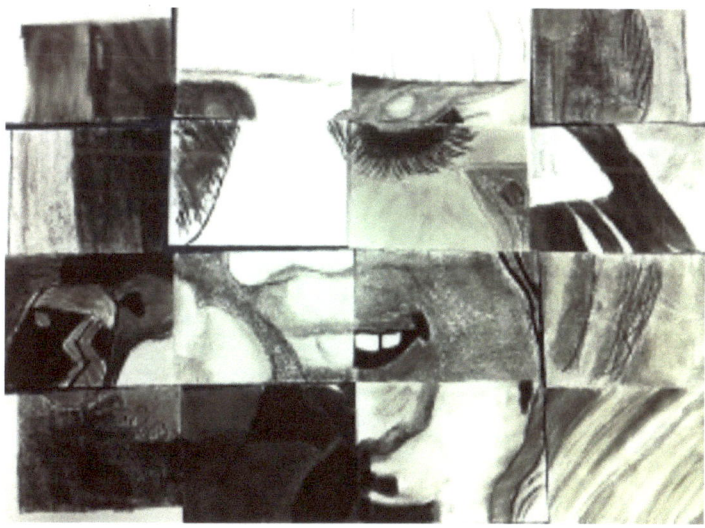

Here's an example of a face created by students. The kids felt so proud of themselves after this, and while they were drawing their section, they had no idea it would turn out to be a face.

After this, give the students an A4 image to copy on their own. Also, give them an A3 cover sheet with a single square cut out. When you place the A3 cover sheet over the A4 image, only a small portion of the image is visible. Then get the students to copy the image onto a blank A4 sheet, one square at a time.

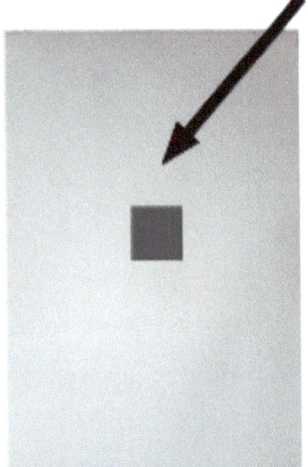

Two sheets of A3 paper with a square cut out. One is to cover the photo the students are copying, and the other is to cover their drawing. They will draw only a square at a time. If necessary, number the squares in the image and on the students' drawing paper to help them keep track of where they are up to.

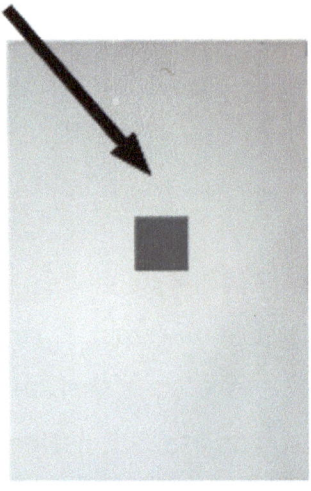

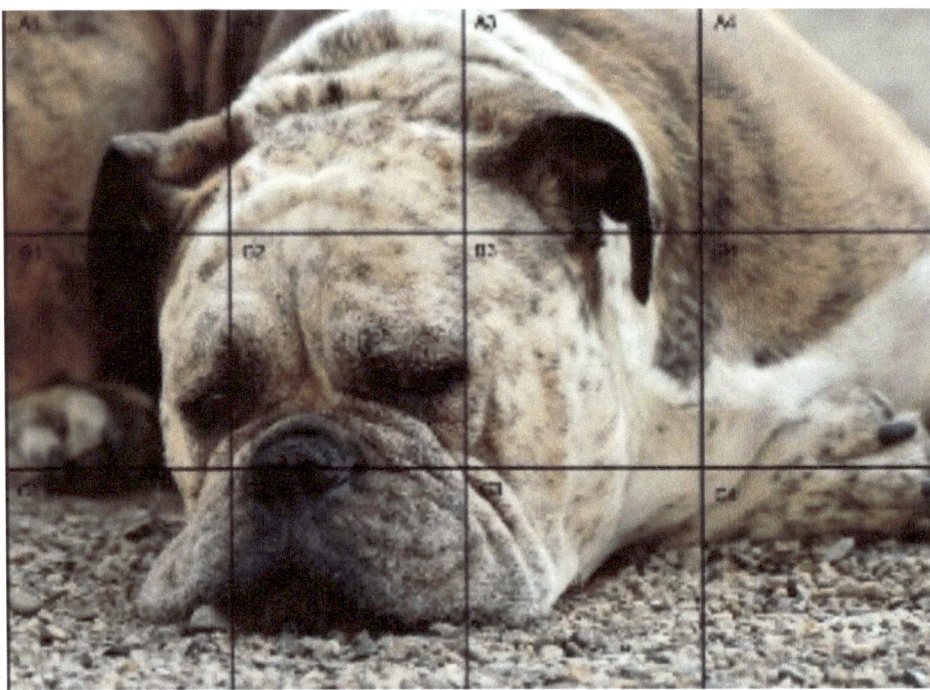

Photo with squares numbered

A1	A2	A3	A4
B1	B2	B3	B4
C1	C2	C3	C4

Paper the students draw on.

They only draw one square at a time and the rest are covered.

A LITTLE MORE SHADING

Give the students a line drawing of a facial profile to copy. This should be relatively easy for them now.

Next, give them a photo that has exactly the same profile, and ask them to shade in their drawing.

If you give them just the photo to start, they consider it harder than if they are given only a line drawing to begin. The brain takes over and has an internal conversation that says it's just too difficult.

Bit by bit we are breaking this down and teaching the brain to see things as a series of shapes, lines and tones...regardless of the subject.

Some methods teach that you can break everything down into a series of shapes.

In some ways, this is true, but I prefer students to learn that every shape is unique - and to carefully observe the lines and contours of what they are looking at specifically.

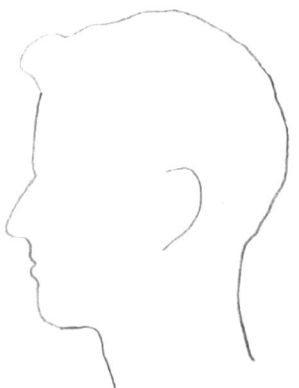 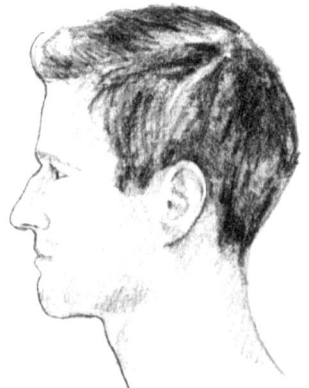

Animals are wonderful to draw as well, so get the students to draw some animal profiles in the same way.

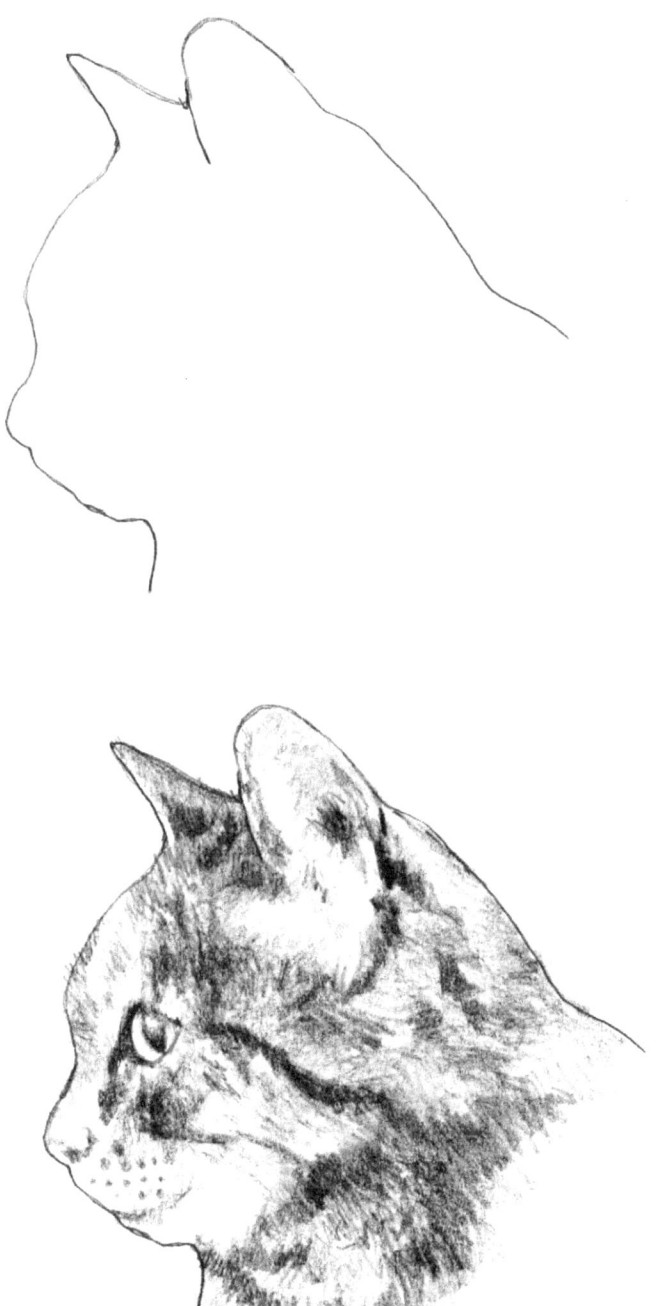

30

CROSS REFERENCE
MEASURING

Everything has a size with respect to the things around it - and also components within it. Learning to automatically cross-reference where something is in relation to other things, will be the primary way you get measurements correct.

Start the students with a series of objects to draw that go down in size. Get them to pay attention to where they are in relation to each other as they draw them.

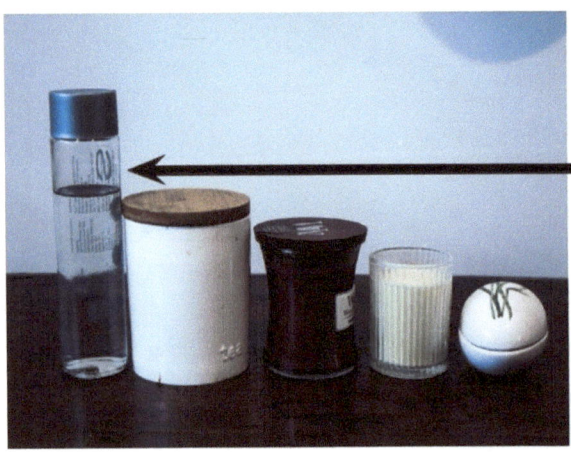

The second canister comes about two-thirds up the first skinny one. Do this comparison for all the other objects.

Then mix up the objects and get them to draw them again. They will now have to cross -reference them with different items, and this exercise will help them to think about the size relationship between objects.

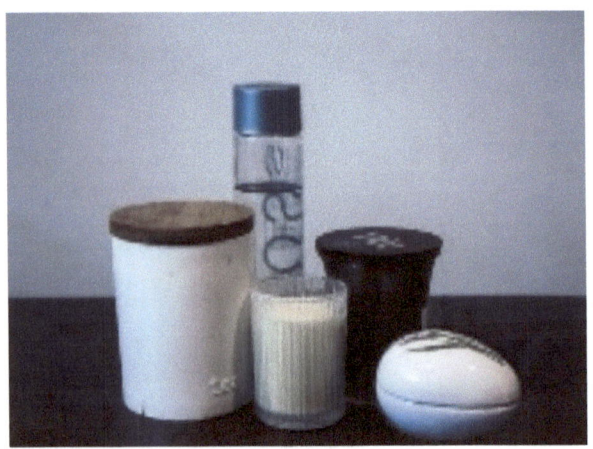

SIGHT-SIZE DRAWING

Hold your ruler (or pencil, or anything straight) out in front of you with your arm fully extended. Close one eye and measure the first bit of the subject you wish to draw. Hold the ruler against the paper and mark that measurement on your paper. Continue this process until you have most of the main points of the drawing down. If you want the drawing to be bigger or smaller, you simply move closer or further away from the subject.

You have to make sure you don't lean in or back when doing this as it can make a difference, and you'll get the measurements incorrect. Always double-check this with cross-reference measurement. It's a handy extra trick and good to know.

With all of these techniques, however, you should always be going back to drawing what you can see and not worrying if it doesn't immediately make sense. And the more you do this, the better you'll get – it's like practising your scales on the piano, although a lot more fun in my humble opinion.

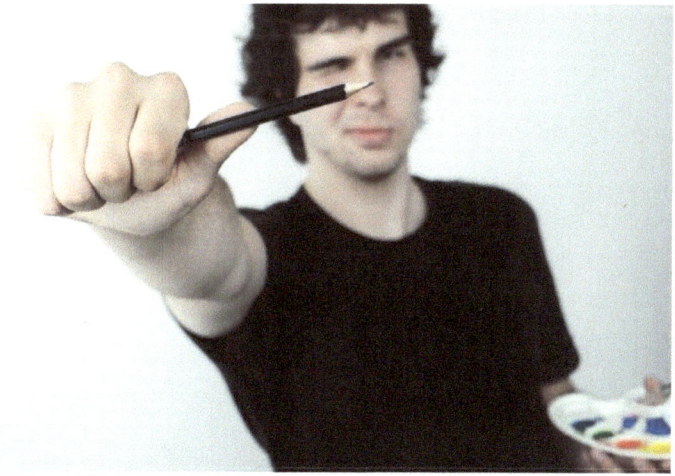

© Velkol | Megapixl.com

NEGATIVE SPACE

The space behind objects is called negative space, and paying attention to this is a brilliant way to check your measuring. The negative space also has shape and dimensions, so by looking at this, you can double -check that your drawing is representing what you are seeing.

Chairs are great things to draw to demonstrate negative space, as well as people in weird poses.

Get the students to draw only the outline of what they are drawing and leave all the interior out.

A good exercise is to get them to trace around in the air with their finger first before they start drawing on the paper.

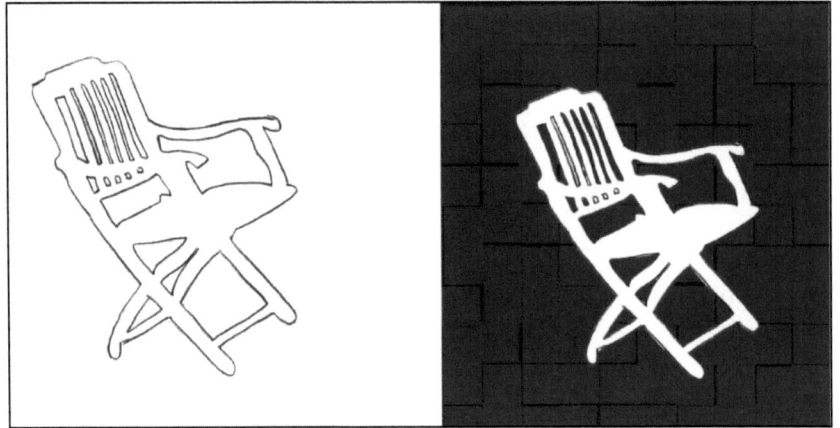

In all the spaces behind the object, get the students to draw some interesting patterns. That way, they are focusing on the negative space and not the actual object.

It's helpful to cross -reference the negative space to check if the proportions are correct. Using the chair example, if the negative space between the arm and the seat of the chair were the wrong size, then you would know that the chair wasn't in proportion yet.

LIGHT AND SHADE

Let's look at light and shade a little more and experiment with creating different lighting effects.

Start with a straightforward still life with a directional light on one side and get the students to draw it focusing on the shading.

Now move the light to show the students that the shading and look of an object are very dependent on the light source. So to presume that there's a single way to draw something makes no sense.

Then move the light overhead and see what happens.

And finally, move it to the other side.

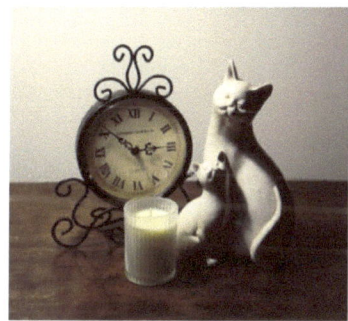
Low left light

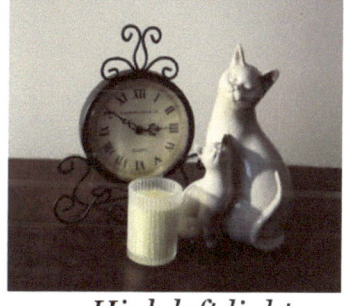
High left light

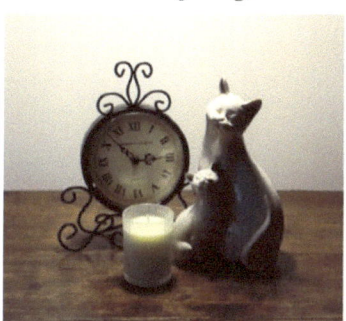
Overhead light

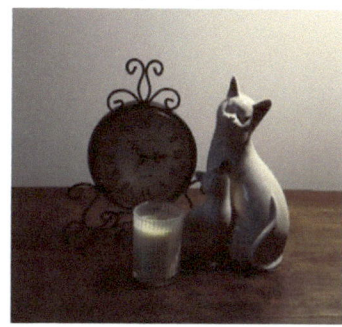
Right side light

For this reason, it's difficult for them to get a realistic result when we tell kids to draw something from their imagination. There are many variations and so much information that we would have to visually remember, so our minds naturally simplify it for us. So when kids reach that critical age of wanting to draw realistically, they get frustrated because they can't do it from their memory, and they haven't practised enough drawing from what's around them.

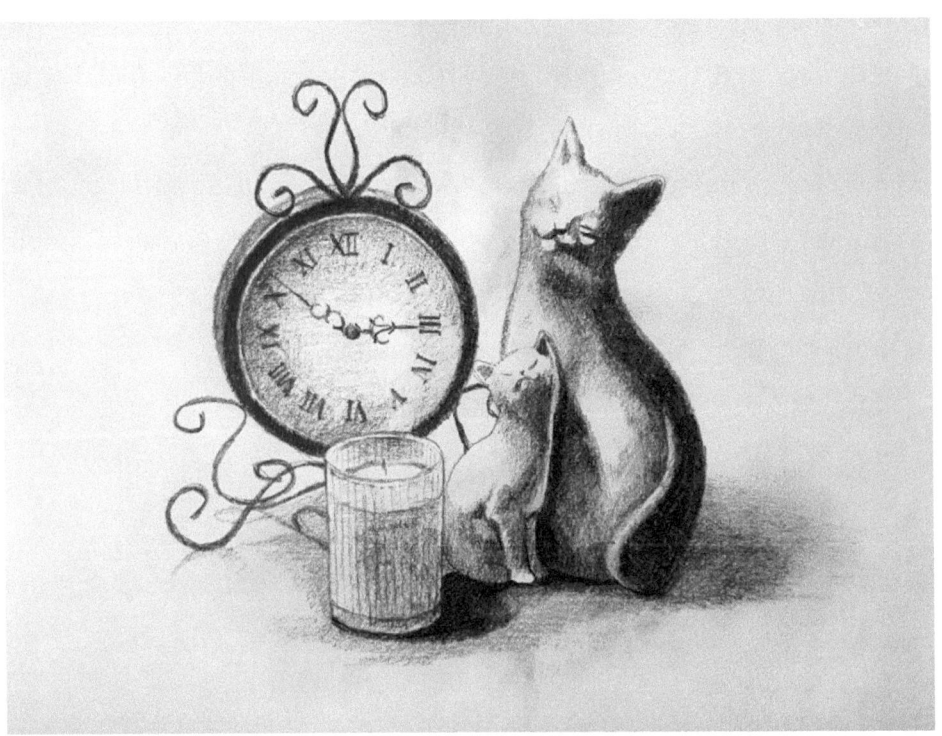

This drawing was from the photo where the light was on the far left side.

LEARNING PROPORTIONS

Learning about proportions is an excellent way to break the preconceived ideas that people sometimes have about how objects look.

A classic example of this is that many people when they first start drawing think that the eyes are much further up the head than they truly are. In reality, they are approximately half-way. A lot of this misinterpretation is due to the hairline which people don't internally count when measuring where the eyes are.

So learning about proportions is a great thing.

BUT...they also have to be prepared to let go of these rules as they are drawing and go back to the old familiar saying...draw what you see.

This is because foreshortening and perspective change the rules. A person who is throwing their head back laughing won't look as if their eyes are in the middle of their head due to foreshortening.

Nonetheless, it's good to learn, and it teaches some basic guidelines for when we are looking at something straight on. And understanding this can also break some internal beliefs about what you might have incorrectly thought something looked like (hands are often bigger than people think, for example).

THE FIGURE

It's generally accepted that the length of the head will fit seven -and-a-half times into the body. The classical proportions were eight heads into the body, but many of those figures were god-like creatures, and not like us humble mortals (although this is still used for fashion models and magazines).

The mid-point is at the pubic bone and not at the waist as most people think. The female form is more rounded with narrower shoulders and wider hips than the male.

Children have different proportions. Toddlers are approximately four heads tall, and seven-year-olds are six heads tall. By the age of ten, they are about seven heads tall.

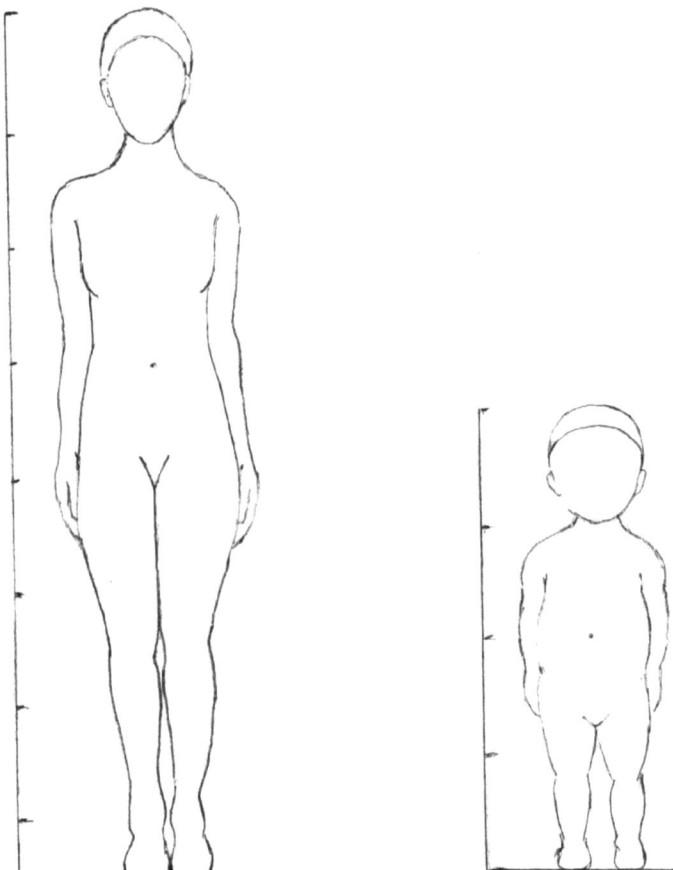

Get the students to draw an outline of themselves on a large piece of paper, or with a whiteboard marker on a full-length glass door or window. Break down the figure into head measurements and get them to look at where everything is in relation to each other.

THE FACE

When the face is viewed straight on it generally has the following qualities:

- The width of the head is about two -thirds the height.
- The eyes are half-way in the middle of the face.
- The bottom of the nose is half-way between the top of the eyes and the bottom of the chin.
- The bottom of the mouth is half-way between the bottom of the nose and the chin.
- The corners of the mouth align with the middle of the eyes.

Photograph the students' faces front on and get them to cross-reference these measurements and see if they match.

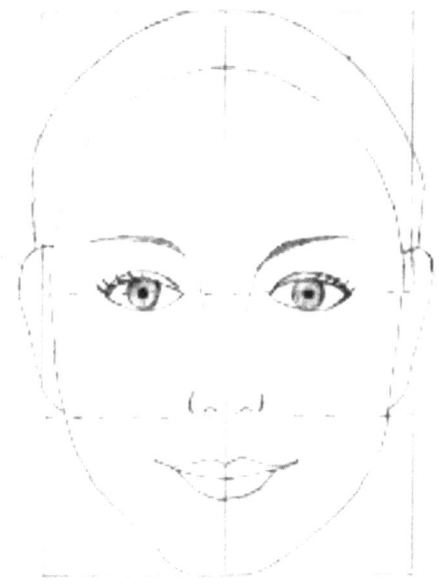

Children and babies have bigger foreheads, and the middle of their eyes is about three-sevenths up the face.

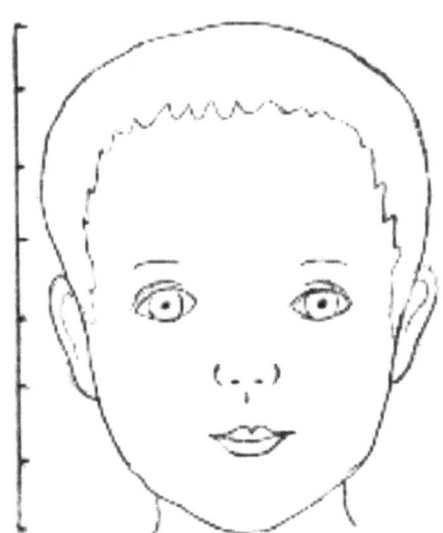

When in profile, the head divides in half at the jawline in front of the ears. The back of the head is deceptively larger than most people think.

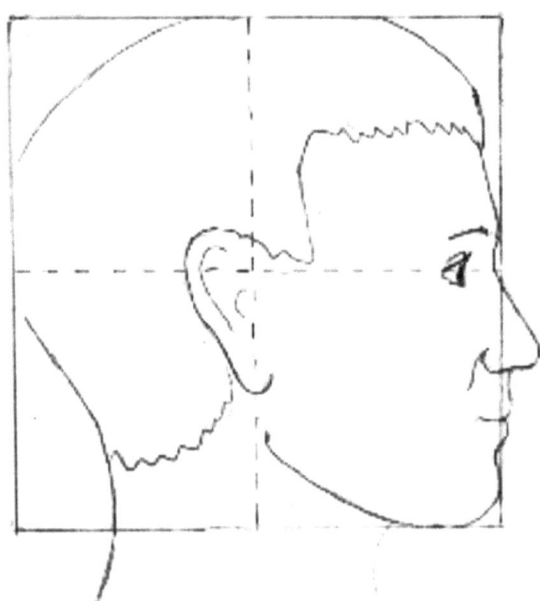

LIGHT AND SHADE ON FACES

Do the same light and shade exercise that we did previously with a still life but this time with a face. It will be fun for the students to see how the light changes the whole mood and emotion of the person.

It's a good introduction to film lighting as well.

Using an artificial light source, illuminate a face from the side, above and below.

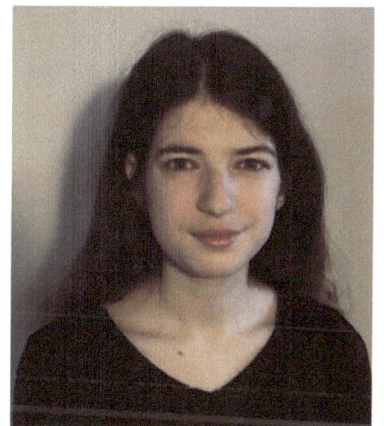
Light front on

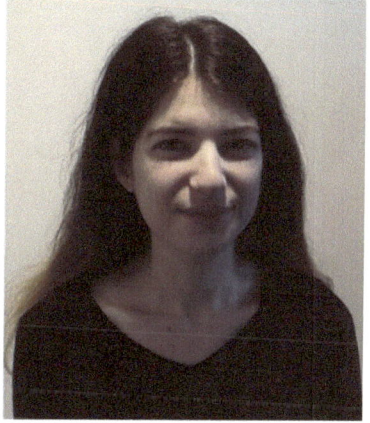
Light overhead

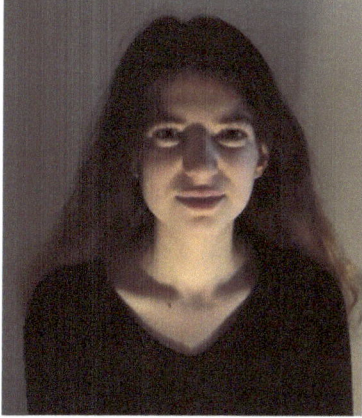
Light underneath

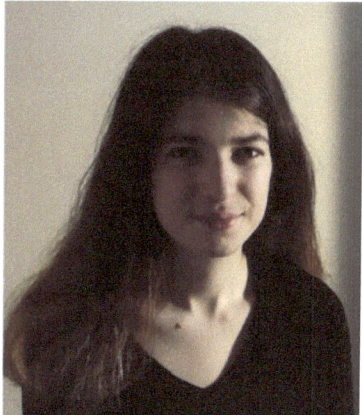
Light to the side

After the students have seen the effect of different artificial lights, have a chat with them about outdoor light. Morning and late afternoon light create lovely sidelight and longer shadows. The light is a little more orange than the middle of the day, and these times are great for portraiture.

In the middle of the day, the sun is directly overhead, and the shadows are much harsher. This time can be great if you want to create something a little gritty. On overcast days the light will be softer and can be quite flattering but with less contrast. When starting out, I would recommend that you choose lighting that has contrast as it will be easier for you to get interesting modelling on your subject.

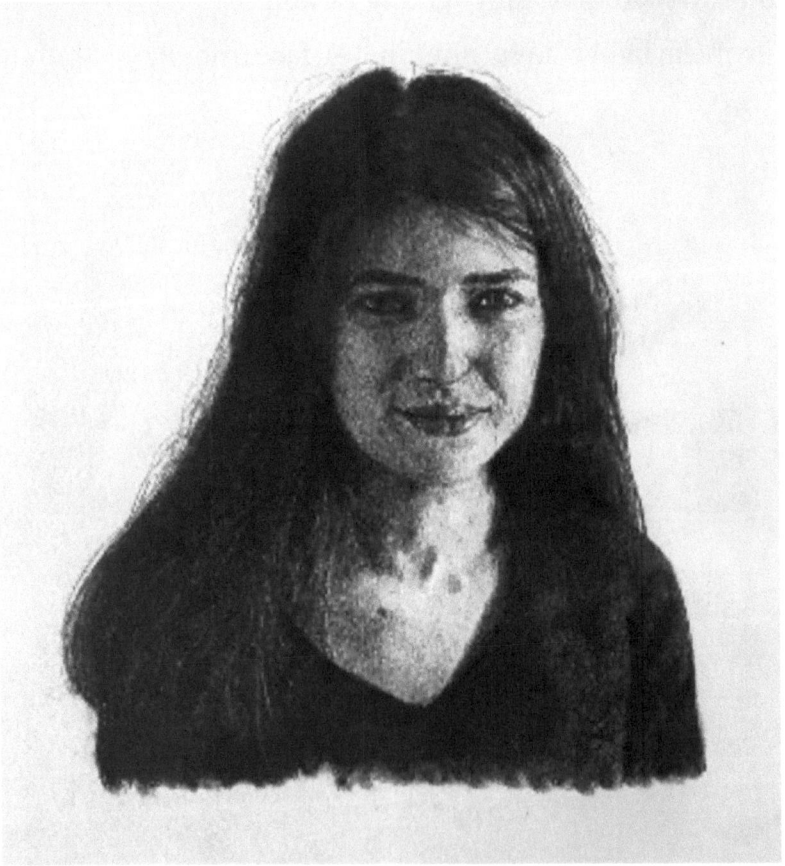

This drawing was done using artificial lighting to the side. It's a great type of light to use as it creates good shadows to draw which give your drawing structure and is also attractive on the subject.

PERSPECTIVE
1 POINT, 2 POINT, AND 3 POINT

Understanding perspective is helpful when drawing realistic three dimensions.

Like many techniques, perspective is important to learn, but shouldn't stop you from drawing what you see and trusting your eyes.

Have you ever noticed how clouds get smaller the further away they go? This is an example of perspective where things diminish and get smaller as they recede into the background.

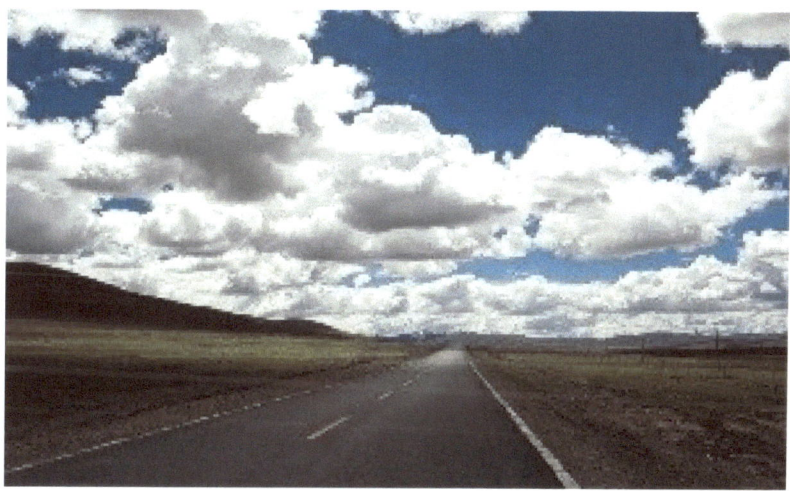

ONE-POINT PERSPECTIVE

A road receding into the distance (such as the example above) is a great example of one-point perspective.

Every line going back on our page is going to follow a path towards a vanishing point which is on the horizon line. The horizon line will be either the horizon or whatever horizontal line is level with your eye. All these lines meet at one point.

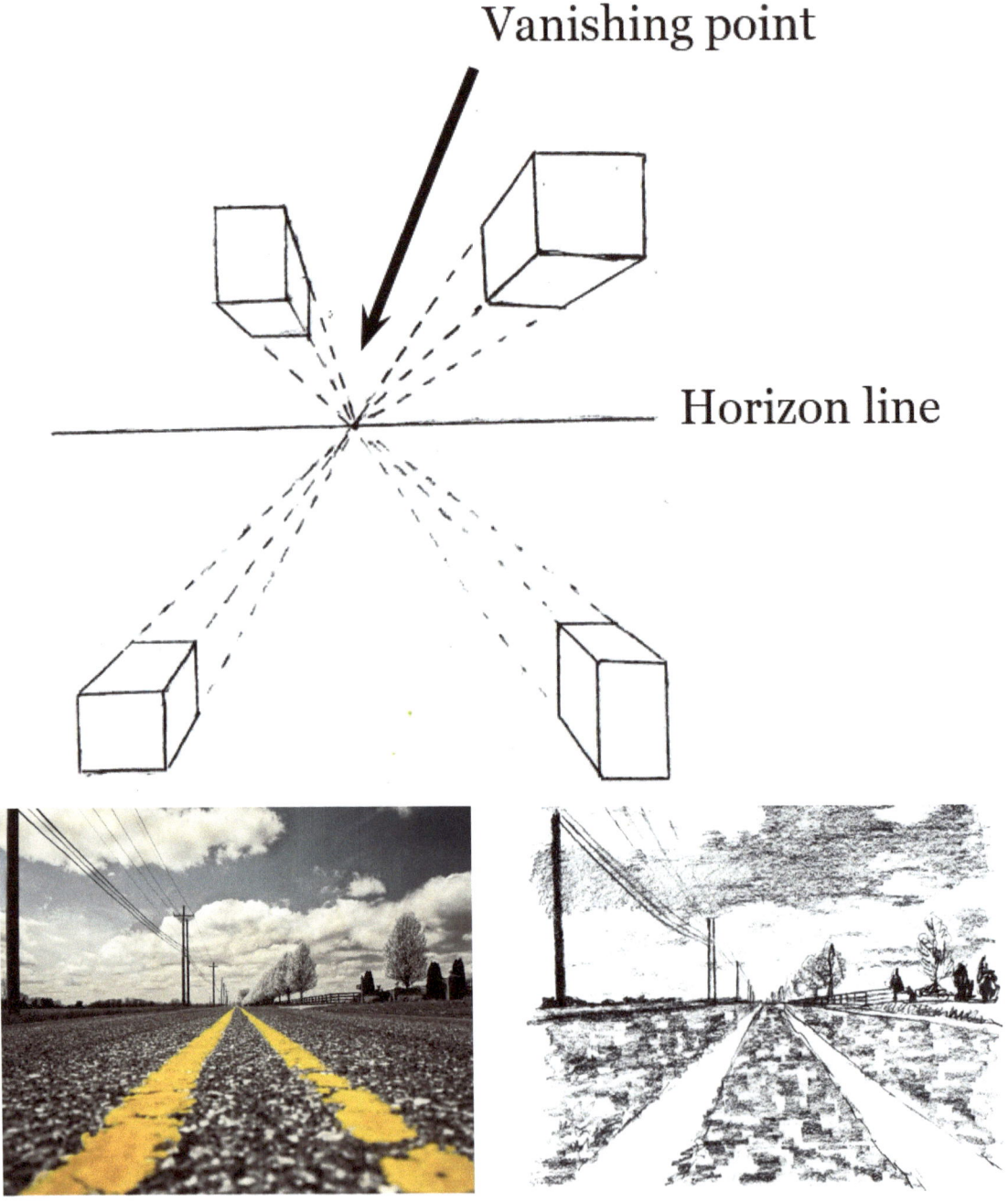

Getting the students to write their name with one-point perspective can be an excellent exercise.

Vanishing point

Horizon line

Here the yellow lines of the road are heading towards the vanishing point in the middle on the horizon line.

TWO-POINT PERSPECTIVE

When an object is in full-frontal, you will see two sides, and this will then have two vanishing points to either side.

Drawing a simple house is a great exercise to practise this.

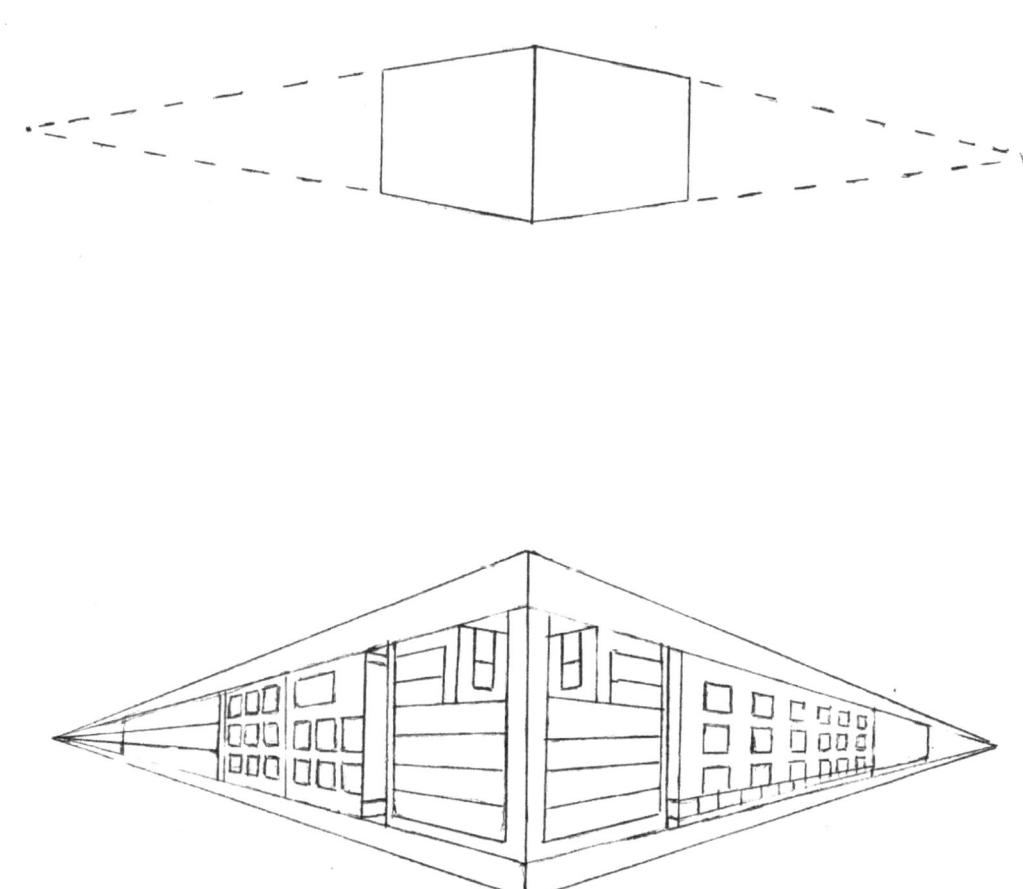

THREE-POINT PERSPECTIVE

If an object is observed from an extreme angle, then the vertical lines will have their own vanishing points as well. This is seen when you're viewing something from very low, or very high.

A city building would be an excellent subject to explore three - point perspective.

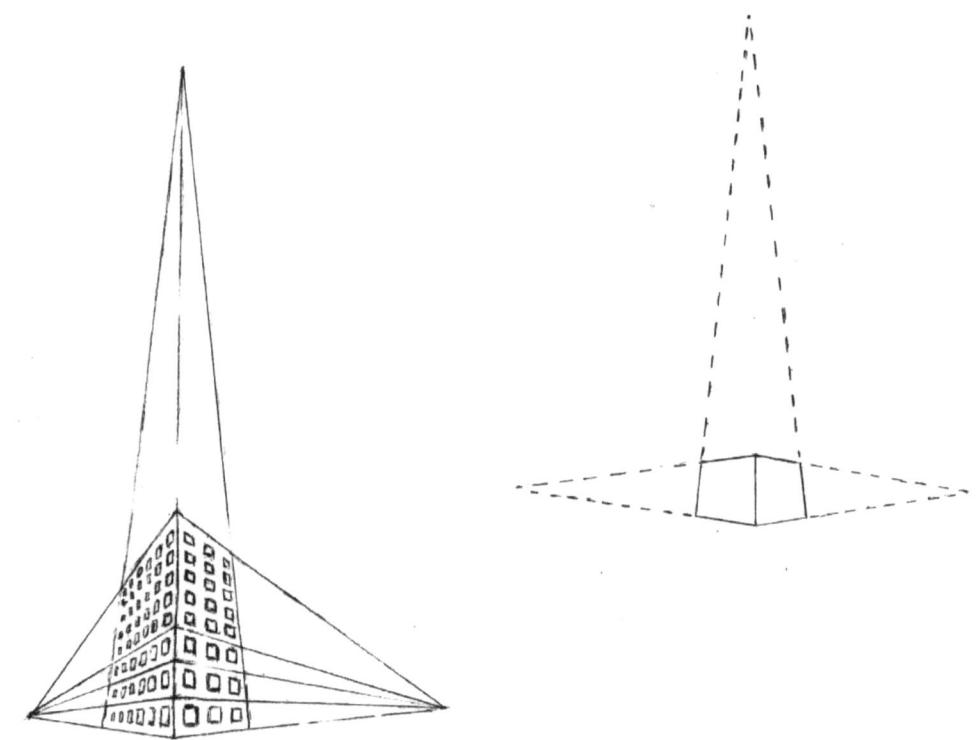

When dealing with younger children, you wouldn't go into two-point or three points perspective a great deal, if at all. However, it's fun to introduce to older students.

SHADOWS
UNDERNEATH AND CAST SHADOWS

Shadows are an important part of adding realism to a drawing. Everything casts a shadow in the opposite direction to the light source. If you have multiple light sources or ambient light, then knowing where the shadow is can be confusing. Luckily our eyes will tell us! Also, be aware that objects cast shadows on other objects, and these are called cast shadows.

Set up a still life for the students with some powerful sidelight. Get the students to draw the still life and concentrate on the shadows and how they are placed and fade out. Look at the edges of the shadows. Consider how some have fuzzier edges depending on how strong the light is.

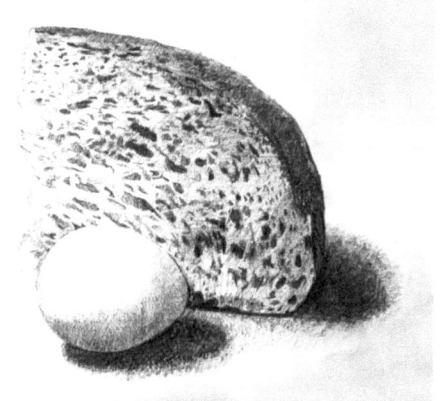

Reference for drawing © Adyoo | Megapixl.com

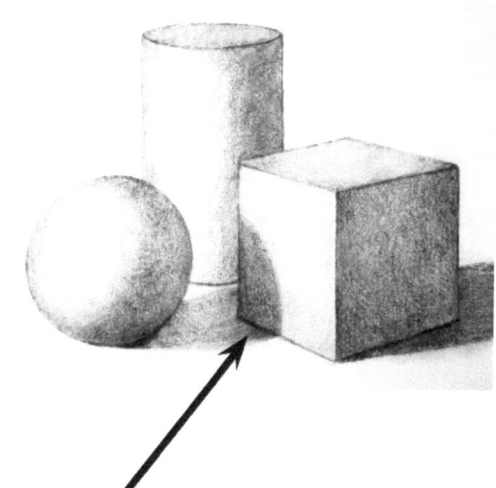

This is an excellent example of a cast shadow from one object onto another.

DIFFERENT TEXTURES

When students are starting to learn to draw, they will think that some textures or objects are more challenging than others.

In reality, nothing is harder than anything else – some subjects just contain more detail.

Bring in photos of a few different objects with different textures, such as a glass or a teddy bear.

Only give the students a section of the photos and ask them to draw that one little square. This way, when they draw the whole thing, a lot of the bias over how difficult a particular texture is will already have diminished.

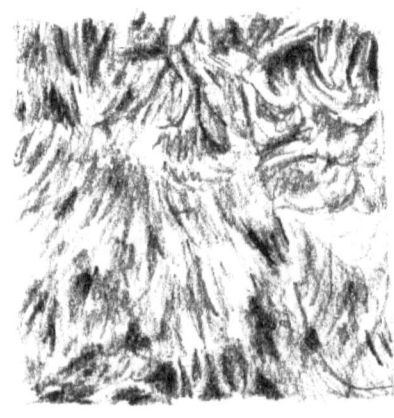

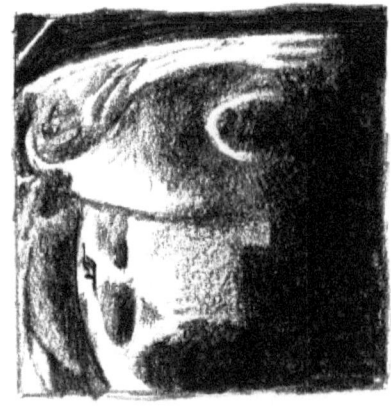

These are the full drawings from the texture sample. Looking at only a piece of the texture makes it easier to see the whole when you come to it.

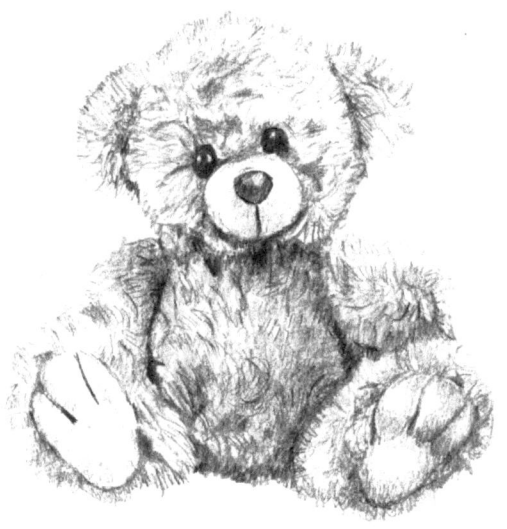

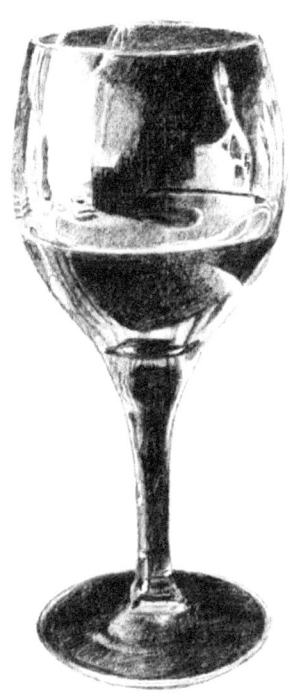

FORESHORTENING

Foreshortening is a technique used to give the illusion of something receding strongly into the distance or background. The illusion is created by the object appearing shorter than it is in reality, making it seem compressed. If you look at the ring here, you'll see how it changes shape depending on what angle we view it. The first image is extremely foreshortened, and all sense of the circle is lost. We know by looking at it though, that it is a circle because of its shape and shading.

Ask the students to draw rings at different angles. Also, get them to shade their drawings as shading will help the foreshortening make sense.

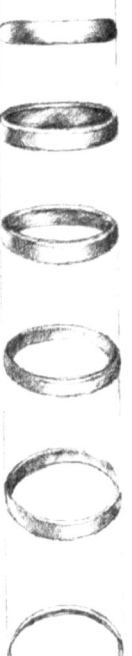

If you asked children to draw a ring, they would automatically draw a circle. But as demonstrated here, a ring doesn't always look like a circle. The very first ring here appears like a curvy band because it's foreshortened. As it turns, it gradually becomes the circle shape that we associate with a ring. Once students realise this and know that they have to look and observe, they have passed a considerable hurdle.

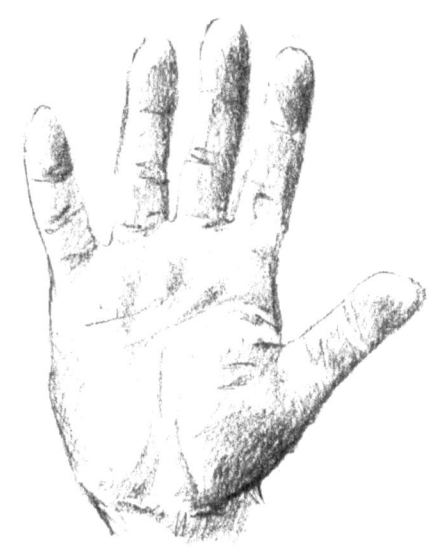

Here is a hand that looks how most people automatically think of a hand. It shows five digits and is straight on to the viewer.

However, hands are very rarely held like this unless you are constantly saying "hi" to people!

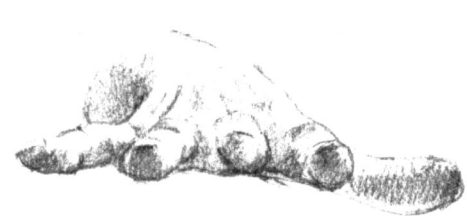

Here is a foreshortened hand. It's nothing like the image one conjures when thinking of a hand.

But encourage the students to know that if it's in front of them, then they have to be brave and draw it. It will all come together in the end.

CONCLUSION

My final words to help anyone of any age to draw realistically is to go back to what you can see. To trust that when you're drawing a super weird shape that seems nothing like you think it should - but is in fact following the lines and measurements of what your 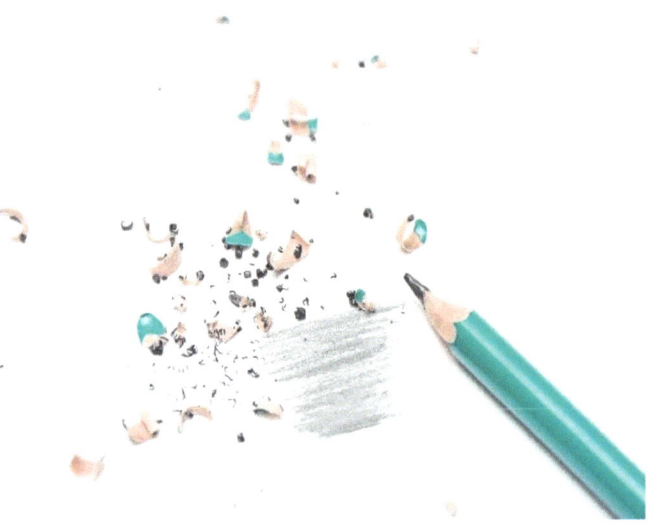 eye is telling you - it is correct. Keep going and trust that it will turn out well in the end ...and the more you do it, the more accurate it will get.

Have fun inspiring the kids to explore. By constantly observing the world around them, they'll be creating masterpieces in no time.

The exercises in this book are wonderful ways for students to develop their ability to draw realistically.

But the main thing is to encourage students to find objects that they would like to draw (or use a photo if they wish at the start) and copy what's in front of them!

Learning to draw realistically will develop skills in your students beyond being able to create a visually pleasing artwork. The process of drawing realistically can make kids more alert and sensitive to all the details in the world that they may otherwise miss.